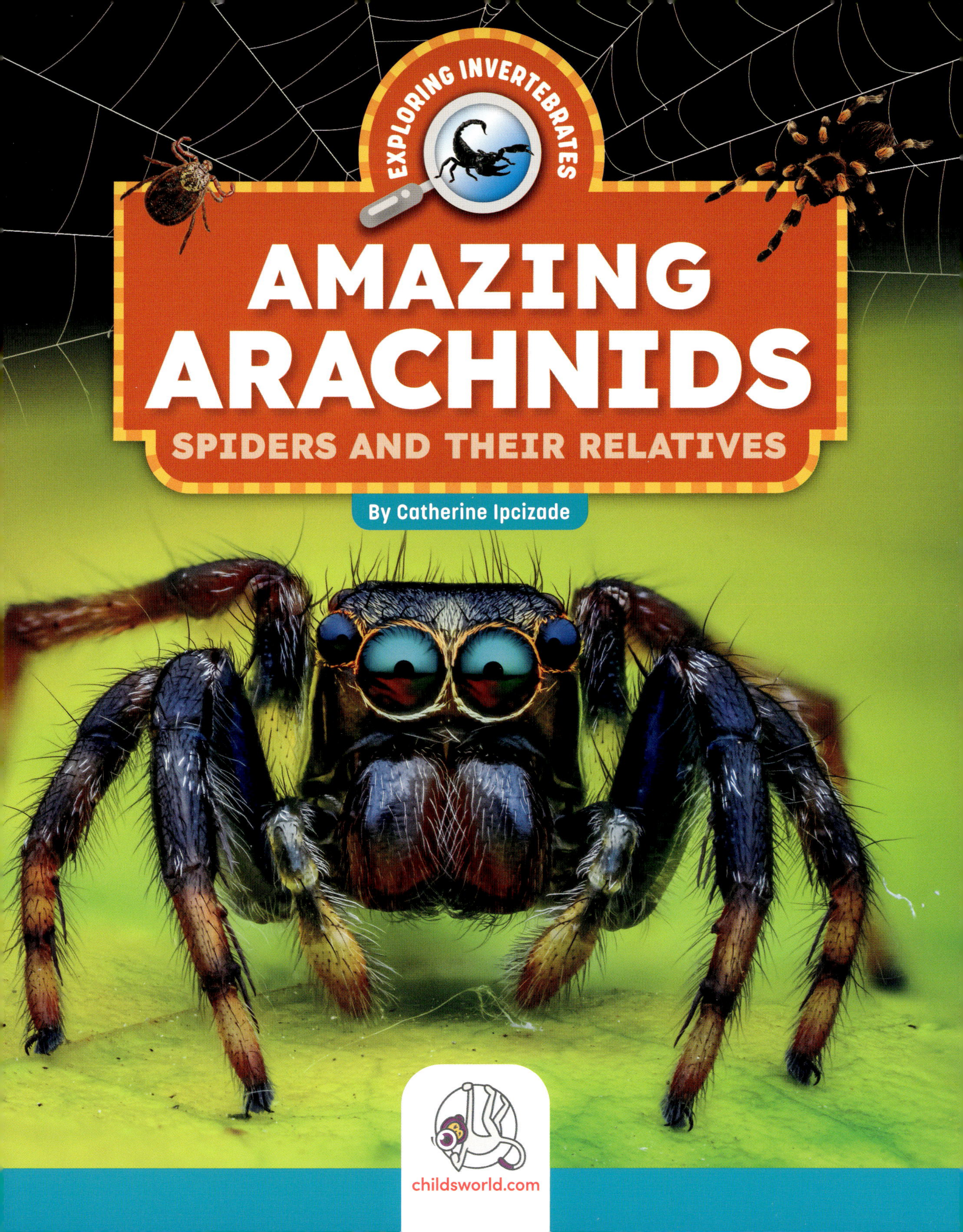
EXPLORING INVERTEBRATES
AMAZING ARACHNIDS
SPIDERS AND THEIR RELATIVES
By Catherine Ipcizade
childsworld.com

Published by The Child's World®
800-599-READ • childsworld.com

Photography Credits
Cover: ©nechaevkon/Shutterstock; Kurit afshen/Shutterstock; Ernie Cooper/Shutterstock; ©Reynold Tjandi/Shutterstock; ©Tran The Ngoc/Shutterstock; page 3: ©Alfred Evelina/500px/Getty Images; Audrey Snider-Bell/Shutterstock; pages 4–5: ©Lions/E+/Getty Images; page 5: ©Kaiskynet Studio/Shutterstock; ©Goldfinch4ever/iStock/Getty Images; ©nechaevkon/Shutterstock; ©QAI Publishing/Universal Images Group/Getty Images; ©Pamela Au/Shutterstock; page 7: ©Mikhail Egorov/Shutterstock; page 8: ©Tobias Hauke/Shutterstock; ©Alongkot Sumritjearapol/Moment/Getty Images; page 9: ©Arzell/Shutterstock; pages 10–11: ©Elva Etienne/Moment/Getty Images; page 12: ©Sebastian Kaulitzki/Science Photo Library/Getty Images; page 13: ©Niney Azman/Shutterstock; page 14: ©Blue Ring Media/Shutterstock; ©Shashidharswamy Hiremath/Shutterstock; page 15: ©nechaevkon/Shutterstock; pages 16–17: ©Sonia Nadales/Shutterstock; pages 18–19: ©Peter Finch/Stone/Getty Images; page 19: ©TaufikPho/Shutterstock; page 20: ©photoJS/Shutterstock; page 21: ©Audrey Snider-Bell/Shutterstock; page 22: ©Heather Williams/personal; page 23: ©Goldfinch4ever/iStock/Getty Images; page 24: ©Alfred Evelina/500px/Getty Images

ISBN Information
9781503894488 (Reinforced Library Binding)
9781503894730 (Portable Document Format)
9781503895553 (Online Multi-user eBook)
9781503896376 (Electronic Publication)

LCCN
2024942887

Printed in the United States of America

ABOUT THE AUTHOR

Catherine Ipcizade is a college professor and the author of more than 30 books for children. She loves photography, cooking, and spending time with her family in sunny California and the mountains of Utah. Her favorite word is "serendipity" because life is full of unexpected, fortunate surprises.

CONTENTS

MEET THE ARACHNIDS!

A wolf spider eats dozens of aphids on a rose bush. The aphids would have destroyed the plant. The spider gets a meal, and a plant is saved. Spiders are arachnids. There are more than 100,000 **species** of arachnids. Spiders make up the largest group. But they aren't the only arachnids (uh-RAK-nidz). Harvesters, scorpions, mites, and ticks are also arachnids. They are part of the largest group of animals, the **invertebrates**.

Arachnids come in many shapes and sizes. Mites are so tiny that people need a microscope to see them. Harvesters have tiny bodies and long legs. Scorpions are a bit bigger, from the size of a paper clip to the size of an adult hand. And spiders can be small or large.

SOME COMMON ARACHNIDS:

scorpion

spider

tick

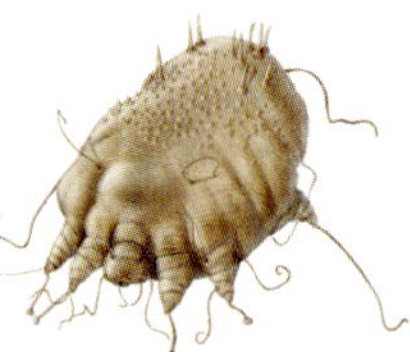

mite

harvester

About 50,000 types of spiders have been discovered. They can be as small as a pinhead, or as large as a dinner plate!

Just as arachnids look different, they also eat different foods. Spiders might nibble a tiny insect or worm. Larger spiders might even eat a frog or a bat! Scorpions are hunters that eat whatever they can grab. Other arachnids aren't quite so adventurous. Harvesters eat insects, rotting fruit or mushrooms, or animal droppings. Mites are sometimes **scavengers**. That means they eat **decaying** meat or rotting plants. Others eat insects such as ants. And ticks feed off of hosts. That means they attach their bodies to mammals, reptiles, fish, and birds, and they eat by sucking their blood. Ticks often find a different host for each stage of their lives.

For most arachnids, anywhere can be called home. They live all over the world. Some spiders even live in the water. Scorpions are often found in the desert. Some scorpions prefer to live in caves. Harvesters like moist environments. That's why they are sometimes found stretching their long legs in the bathtub.

Scorpions can be found on every continent except Antarctica.

MAGNIFICENT SCORPIONS

Scorpions can survive for months without food or water. Some scorpions can even survive eating only one insect per year! That's because scorpions can **hibernate**. Scorpions use their pincers to squeeze **prey**. Digestive fluids inside their mouths break down the food. They get their food and much of their water this way.

A CLOSER LOOK

Arachnids are arthropods. They have eight legs and no antennae. Their bodies are divided into two parts—a cephalothorax (sef-uh-loh-THOR-aks) and an abdomen. The cephalothorax includes the head and neck. Since arachnids are invertebrates, they don't have backbones. They have flexible yet strong **exoskeletons** to support their bodies.

Many arachnids, including spiders and scorpions, have multiple eyes. Some have no eyes at all. Some have up to 12 eyes.

Spiders and scorpions don't have noses. They breathe out of book lungs. These lungs look like the thin pages of a book. They are located on the arachnid's abdomen.

LET'S TAKE A LOOK!

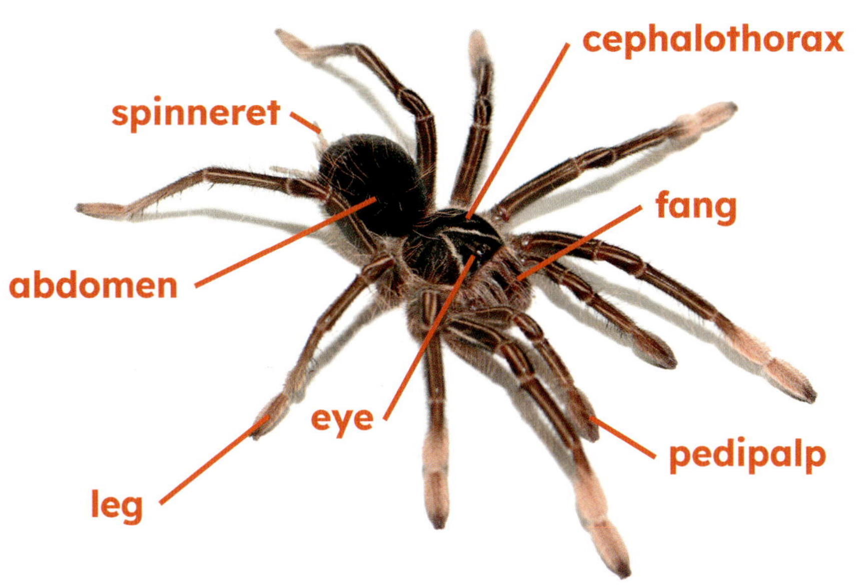

Many arachnids have unique abilities. A spider uses silk from its **spinneret** to weave a web that is stronger than steel. Spiders use webs to catch prey and also to build shelter or to protect their eggs. When a scorpion senses danger, it gives off a special glowing light called **biofluorescence** that scares the predator away. Spiders and scorpions also use **venom** to sting prey. But not all arachnids are venomous.

Being a mighty arachnid often means living alone. They may form groups to mate, but few arachnids enjoy the company of others. Spiders might attack each other if forced to socialize. The exception is a group of spiders called social spiders. These spiders thrive on living in a community. They build webs together and even hunt together. Harvesters often socialize with other harvesters around water. But for the most part, arachnids live and work best by themselves.

NO SPIDERS HERE

Harvesters are often mistaken for spiders. They look like spiders. They have long legs that push their small bodies forward. But they do not have silk glands. That means they don't spin webs. Some harvesters do not have eyes, and some have only two eyes. Spiders, on the other hand, can have no eyes or up to 12 eyes.

Harvesters are often referred to as daddy longlegs. They are often mistaken for cellar spiders because of their attraction to cool, dark places.

LIFE CYCLE

Unlike some invertebrates that go through **metamorphosis**, arachnids go through incomplete metamorphosis. That means they begin life looking like tiny versions of their adult selves. Then they grow and grow. Arachnids do this by **molting**. They shed their exoskeleton as they get bigger. Spiders and scorpions molt at least five times between birth and adulthood.

Being a mite means having a short lifespan. Most mites only live a day or two. But some mites live up to eight weeks if they are feeding on humans.

Other arachnids live longer. Ticks and some types of harvesters live for two to three years. Spiders and scorpions may live for a few days or up to 30 years or longer depending on the species and its home. In fact, scorpions are one of the longest-lasting creatures on the planet. They were on Earth before dinosaurs.

Scorpions can molt up to six times, while some spiders molt 12 times before becoming full-grown.

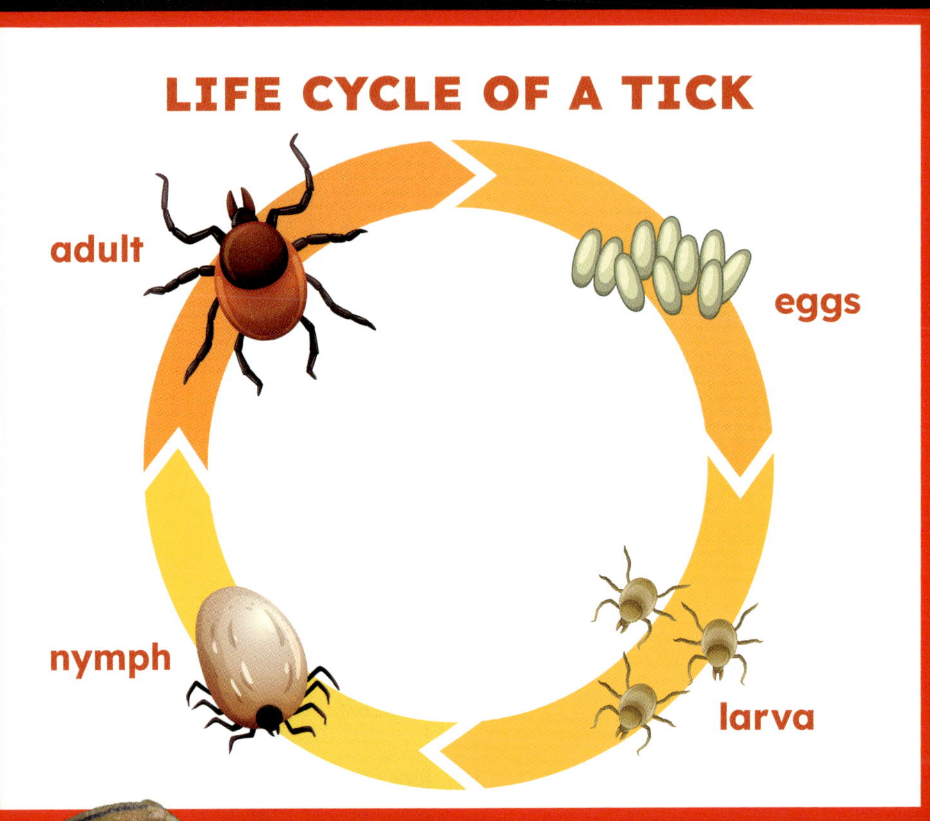

Most scorpions give birth to between 20 and 50 babies at a time. Some larger scorpions can have up to 100!

ALL AROUND US

Mites are everywhere! Almost every plant has at least three mites, but because mites are so small, they are almost impossible to see. Mites are found on humans, animals, insects, mammals, and in oceans and soil. Some mites are pests. Other mites are important contributors to our planet.

Spiders, mites, ticks, and harvesters all lay eggs. A house mite may lay up to three eggs each day. Spiders can lay hundreds of eggs at a time. No wonder they make up the largest group of arachnids! The only arachnid that lays more eggs than a spider is a tick. Ticks lay thousands of eggs.

Scorpions don't lay eggs at all. They give birth to broods of babies, called scorplings. Scorpions carry their babies around on their backs until they are strong enough to survive on their own.

ARACHNIDS IN THE WORLD

Though humans might scream or run when an arachnid is near, many are tiny heroes of the planet. They are often decomposers. Mites are the mightiest decomposers of all. They help control the insect population and break down nutrients in soil to help crops grow.

Arachnids are also an important part of the food chain. Not only do they eat harmful insects, but they are also prey themselves. Birds, lizards, and frogs eat arachnids to keep their species alive and reproduce.

Spiders are a high-protein food option for many birds, including robins, wrens, and woodpeckers.

Scorpions use their crab-like front pincers and their venomous tail to catch and kill prey.

Scorpions, along with spiders, play a very important role in keeping our world safe and our food growing. As **predators**, they eat insects that can destroy plants. This saves gardens and crops.

CHAPTER 5

KEEPING ARACHNIDS SAFE

It is important for humans to be aware of their surroundings and to know which arachnids can be harmful. Ticks often carry diseases that can harm people and animals. Mites might cause harm to people or plants. Spiders or scorpions might sting a human. But many of these powerful creatures are more helpful than they are scary. Without them, crops might die and our food chain would suffer. It is important to stay cautious and safe around arachnids. But it is just as important to think twice before squashing these eight-legged creatures. Without them, the world would not be the same.

WONDER MORE

Wondering About New Information

How much did you know about arachnids before you read this book? What new information did you learn? Write down two facts that you learned. What surprised you about those facts?

Wondering How It Matters

Spiders spin silky webs to catch prey. Why is this important? What would happen to plants if spiders did not eat insects?

Wondering Why

Why do you think living alone is important for most arachnids? Why do you think some animals can't get along with others?

Ways to Keep Wondering

After reading this book, what questions do you have about arachnids? Which arachnids would you like to learn more about? What can you do to learn more about them?

MAKE A SPIDER!

Create a crawling spider with this fun craft!

Steps to Take

1) Paint your paper plate a dark color of your choice. Allow paint to dry.

2) Cut out a circle and eight legs from black paper.

3) Glue the spider legs onto the circle. Add googly eyes or draw eyes onto your spider.

4) Draw a spider web onto your paper plate with the white crayon.

5) Cut a 1-inch slit in the paper plate. Ask an adult to help you!

6) Glue the craft stick onto the back of the spider. Poke the craft stick through the front of the paper plate into the hole you cut.

7) Hold the plate in one hand and use your other hand to make your spider "crawl" around its web!

Supplies

- paper plate
- popsicle stick
- dark-colored paint
- white crayon
- scissors
- googly eyes (optional)

GLOSSARY

biofluorescence (by-oh-flor-ES-ents) Creatures that have biofluorescence absorb light and then emit it from their bodies, causing them to glow.

decaying (dee-KAY-ing) Decaying means rotting.

exoskeletons (eks-oh-SKELL-uh-tunz) Exoskeletons are hard outer shells invertebrates wear instead of having a backbone.

hibernate (HY-bur-nayt) When an animal hibernates, it spends a long period of time in a deep sleep.

invertebrates (in-VER-tuh-bruts) Invertebrates are animals that do not have a backbone.

metamorphosis (met-uh-MOR-fuh-sis) Metamorphosis is the process of growing from a baby to adult in animals.

molting (MOLT-ing) Molting occurs when an invertebrate sheds its hard exoskeleton in order to grow bigger.

predators (PRED-uh-turs) Predators are creatures that get food by killing and eating other organisms.

prey (PRAY) Prey is an animal that is hunted for food.

scavengers (SKA-ven-jurs) Scavengers are animals that eat decaying meat or rotten plants.

species (SPEE-sheez) A species is a group of living things that are able to reproduce.

spinneret (spin-ur-ETT) A spinneret is an organ that produces a spider's silk.

venom (VENN-uhm) Venom is a poisonous liquid in some animals, including scorpions, that is used to sting or kill prey.

FIND OUT MORE

In the Library

Cowles, Jillian. *Amazing Arachnids.* Princeton, NJ: Princeton University Press, 2018.

Markle, Sandra. *Ticks: An Augmented Reality Experience.* Minneapolis, MN: Lerner, 2021.

Platnick, Norman I. et al. *Spiders of the World: A Natural History.* London, England: Ivy Press, 2020.

On the Web

Visit our website for links about arachnids:
childsworld.com/links

Note to Parents, Caregivers, Teachers, and Librarians: We routinely verify our web links to make sure they are safe and active sites. So encourage your readers to check them out!

INDEX